WIT
for Macn
11.11.01 –

What was it for,
that War to End Wars?
It was for us.
It was for you and yours.

Acknowledgements

Thanks are due to the editors of the *Times Literary Supplement*, in which an early version of the poem 'War Poet' appeared, and of the Greville Press, who published the present version as a pamphlet in association with the Black Jasmine Press, USA. Apart from that title-poem, the dedication, and 'Self-Portrait in Snow', the contents of this book are taken from my *Rounding the Horn: Collected Poems* (1998) and *Body Language* (2004).

Contents

No Ordinary Sunday   9

Home Thoughts from Abroad 1955   11

A Round   14

War Story   15

The Anzac Sonata   16

Apollinaire Trepanned   24

Edward Thomas's Fob Watch   25

War Poet   26

Goodbye to Wilfred Owen   33

War Song of the Embattled Finns   34

A Letter from Berlin   35

Wiedersehen   37

At St Gennys   39

The Nutcracker   41

A poem about Poems About Vietnam   50

A Portrait of Robert Capa   51

Kathmandu–Kodari   52

Skyhorse   53

Self-Portrait in Snow   73

Notes   74

No Ordinary Sunday

No ordinary Sunday. First the light
falling dead through dormitory windows blind
with fog; and then, at breakfast, every plate
stained with the small, red cotton flower; and no
sixpence for pocket money. Greatcoats, lined
by the right, marched from their pegs, with slow
poppy fires smouldering in one lapel
to light us through the fallen cloud. Behind
that handkerchief sobbed the quick Sunday bell.

A granite cross, the school field underfoot,
inaudible prayers, hymn-sheets that stirred
too loudly in the hand. When hymns ran out,
silence, like silt, lay round so wide and deep
it seemed that winter held its breath. We heard
only the river talking in its sleep:
until the bugler flexed his lips, and sound
cutting the fog cleanly like a bird,
circled and sang out over the bandaged ground.

Then, low-voiced, the headmaster called the roll
of those who could not answer; every name
suffixed with honour – 'double first', 'kept goal
for Cambridge' – and a death – in Spitfires, tanks,
and ships torpedoed. At his call there came through
the mist blond heroes in broad ranks
with rainbows struggling on their chests. Ahead
of us, in strict step, as we idled home
marched the formations of the towering dead.

November again, and the bugles blown
in a tropical Holy Trinity,
the heroes today stand further off, grown
smaller but distinct. They flash no medals, keep
no ranks: through *Last Post* and *Reveille*
their chins loll on their chests, like birds asleep.

Only when the long, last note ascends
upon the wings of kites, some two or three
look up: and have the faces of my friends.

1962

Home Thoughts from Abroad
1955

'The finest blades in Rome',
he told my father that first morning, 'come
from this forge. Give me a lump of your
Etruscan, Roman, Syracusan ore
and in ten years I'll have a sword for you
fit for the Emperor's side.' Scuffing a new
sandal in father's shadow, I worried
that riddle round my head – and have carried
it since like a burr. He said: 'I needn't tell
you, sir, there's more than good metal
to a good sword.' I was to learn how much.

The firing, first:
                 'If a cohort can march
thirty miles in battle-order – full pack
and tools – you can walk to the baths and back
like men, not slaves.' 'Centurion, how many
miles did you march in Germany?'
If some doubted his rank, none could deny
his scars: the blue grave on his thigh
of splinters from a Parthian lance; his arms
notched with a tally of battles, night alarms,
ambushes – 'road, river, *our* line, *their* line'
sketched in the schoolyard sand. The Cisalpine
frontier burned at our backs, and its ash fell
on Rome that year and the next year as well;
ash freighting every wind, blighting one roof
in ten. The mothers of my friends wore grief
and Gaius, Marcus, and Marcellus missed
a week of school. Whenever the rest
played Romans and Barbarians, those three
would not draw lots for Spartacus and Pompey,
Caesar and Vercingetorix.
                 The years
brought back from their resonant frontiers

proconsular heroes, whose names were cut
across the blackened benches where we sat
to hear them speak of Rome... of her galleys
and viaducts as the earth's arteries
flowing with grain and metal... and of work
to be done in the eagles' endless wake.

From fire to anvil:
                                over an iron knee
we learnt the rule of law. Justice decreed
three hammer blows for bad hexameters,
four for disrespect to gods or ancestors,
five for disloyalty, six for deceit,
and one for flinching when the hammer beat.

From fire to anvil, anvil to water –
breaking its skin each morning in winter
to steel our own against the furious
skies of the frontiers awaiting us.
The frontiers of the body we pushed back,
wrestling, mapped them on the running track,
until we ruled ourselves; until, after
ten years, we were the men our fathers were.
But fired, forged, tempered, and tested, when we looked
for eagles to follow, all were plucked
naked by northern winds.
                                Today my state,
though not proconsular, is fortunate
enough. For National Servicemen with time
to kill, better the White Man's Grave than tame
parades beside the Rhine or 'bull' at home.
We do no good here and we do no harm,
as they did both, whose colours still at dawn
we hoist above the palms, at dusk haul down.
Come 'Independence', those will be laid up,
and the last legionaries played to their ship
by Hausa bugles, Ibo fifes. When quit
of us, they'll come to blows, but now all's quiet
on the Western Frontier.
                                Tomorrow,

I'm Duty Officer; tonight, must borrow
some Regular's sword for my Sam Browne.
You wonder what the sword's for? Pulling down
thunderbox lids that nobody cleans
in the Royal West African Frontier Force latrines.

1968

A Round

Lead ore lifted from a Cornish mine,
married in a furnace to Cornish tin,
their one flesh pewter, a barnacled plate
salvaged from the ribs of a ship of the line,
in Cape Town market sold for a florin,
bartered for biltong in the Free State,
a farmer's wedding present for his bride
to shine, until – with the waggon-team
taken, the farm in flames – she cried
as he melted it down, tilting its gleam
to the lips of his bullet-mould, one
of whose slugs would open a seam
in a Cornish miner's son.

1999

War Story

of one who grew up at Gallipoli
not over months and miles, but in the space
of feet and half a minute. Wading shoreward
with a plague of bullets pocking the sea
he tripped, as it seemed to him over his scabbard,
and stubbed his fingers on a dead man's face.

1963

The Anzac Sonata

for my uncle Ramsay Howie, *violinist*
    in memory
of his brother Bill Howie, *rifleman*, 1892–1915
and his sister Peggy Howie, 1908–1980

     Another time,
        another place.
     Glossy as a conker
        in its cushioned case.

     Lift and tighten
        the horsehair bow,
     shuttle rosin
        to and fro.

     Hold the note
        there, that first note
     jubilant from
        the fiddle's throat.

I

She remembered the singing. No voice
that she knew and no words, but a cadence,
the speech of a heart with cause to rejoice.

But tell me, now sitting in silence,
with never more cause for grief,
never such darkness, such distance

between us, whether beyond belief
that speech is your speech and yours
that cause for rejoicing. And if,

beyond time, that cadence continues,
send me the jubilant echo
that came to you sixty-five years

ago. Your pen in my hand will know
the note. Its slender antenna inclines
and straightens, leans to the wall, the window.

Another time. I must learn the lines
of a window growing in a dark wall
and listen, as she, to the sibilant pines

and beyond, the approach, lapse, and withdrawal
of surf, off the Bluff, at the world's end.
Then nearer, clearer, the call
of a vibrant string. Turning as she listened,

     one cheek on the pillow
     brushed a cooler cheek
     of fragrant calico.
     Could no more – staring – speak
     than that dumb angel now
     descended here – but how –
     from the toyshop window.

     Hearing the string once more
     sing out, carried my – Nell –
     to Ramsay's room. The door
     was open. Dawnlight fell
     on bow, hand, and fiddle.
     Where did they come from?
                   Bill.
     Bill going to the War.

She remembered the drumming, a pulse in the ear
as of pounding blood, a fever shaking
schoolroom windows. She could not hear

the teacher, though her mouth was making
shapes. The drumming coming. The bell
breaking in, and as suddenly dumb.

Asphalt underfoot. She was holding Nell
in one hand; in the other, the cold
blade of a railing. The drumswell

swept past her leopardskin and gold,
pistons pumping thunder, and Bill
on his bay under a flag enscrolled

Otago Mounted Rifles. Then the bell
told the playground that the show
was over but, shoulder high, Nell
was still waving white calico.

    Five railings down
        watching the bay
    glossy as a conker
        saunter away,

    groomed tail swaying
        to and fro. Lift
    and tighten
        the horsehair bow.

    Hold the note,
        the band's grand tune.
    Hands must cup head
        all afternoon,

    that not a dwindling
        chord be spilled
    until the fiddle
        can be filled.

Good news from Gallipoli: *bought*
my ticket home with a piece of lead
no bigger than a shilling… doctor thought
a bargain… Put the best sheets on his bed.

    Lift and tighten
        the horsehair bow,
    shuttle rosin
        to and fro.

    Hum and rehearse
        each afternoon
    the band's grand
        jubilant tune.

Black news from Gibraltar: *died*
at sea, of fever… towards 5 o'clock,
pulse slackening, he went out with the tide…
We laid him to rest in the shade of the Rock.

    A grave should be in the shade
    of a tree. If we scissored
    a plot in the orchard,
    cut blossom, and made
    a wreath, if you played
    the march and I beat the drum,
    would his spirit not come?

    Another time,
        a brother's face.
    Glossy as a conker
        its cushioned case.

    Lift and tighten
        the horsehair bow.
    Fingers begin,
        horse and hearse follow

> under the bridge
> and varnished arch,
> moving in time
> to the Dead March

Never such darkness, such distance
between them: the one heart stilled
in its case, the other struggling for utterance.

Never such nights and such days filled
with absence – *his* bed, *his* chair – the ache
pervasive as water, and not to be spilled

in words. But stumbling fingers take
comfort from strings that sing
of another time, another place,

of hurts beyond healing, and bring
all into harmony. Music knows
what happens. The hand, bowing,

instructs the heart, as the fiddle grows
with the arm. Fernlike, its coils extend.
Hips widen. The varnish glows

with handling. They speak to each other; friend
confiding in friend, humouring, healing
the hurts. With a horsehair brush in his hand
he paints the air with the colours of feeling.

> Another time,
> a sister's face,
> candle shining
> through Brussels lace.

> Lift and tighten
> the horsehair bow.
> Let petals fly
> and the bells blow

under the bridge
　　　　and varnished arch,
　　dancing to
　　　　the Wedding March.

She remembered the singing, the silence, the face
on the pillow. She heard the jubilant note
another time, another place.

But the angel opened its throat
and mewed for her breast. The sky she saw
reflected in its eyes seems less remote

but bluer, more miraculous than before.
The hands smell sweeter than calico,
and when the feet take to the floor

the first ant drags its shadow
into a garden where the first birds waken.
The beasts are named, and the trees also.

She saw the apple, in its season, taken
and knowing what would follow, drew
an arm through her daughter's when the road was shaken.

She knew the way. The darkness grew
transparent as they walked together.
And, when the dawn came up, she knew
her daughter older than her older brother.

III

'What did the doctor say?' She, on her bed,
could hear her heart drumming. 'He said,
"We've a bit of a battle ahead."'

Not the least cloud troubled the sky.
Heavily burdened, looking ahead,
they moved up the line to die.

Another time,
    another place.
Pack the fiddle
    in its cushioned case.

Lock the door,
    take to the air.
Fiddle and fiddler
    must be there –

picking out
    the band's grand tune
fiery night
    by fiery noon.

A cross-fire nailed them to the cliff
and each dug in, clawing a cave
shaped to the body that rose stiff

at first light, resurrected from its grave.
Trapped in their trenches, shelled and sniped,
with never more cause to grieve

and curse their luck, they grinned, and wiped
back bloody sweat. The steel bees
stung, but only their wounds wept.

Below them, oleanders bloomed in the gullies,
but all who dreamt of gardens woke
to harsher scents than these.

Between barbed wire and prickly oak
they held the line on the place of the skull.
Another morning broke.

In single file, they were moving downhill
and someone was singing. The sky lightened.
She – and an angel – were following Bill
to the beach – and the boat – at the world's end.

Another time,
    another place.
Incline the bow
    above the face

now putting out
    in a cushioned boat,
and paint a garland
    that will float

on the silence
    after her.
At the last stroke
    of the coda,

hold the note
    there, that first note,
jubilant from
    the fiddle's throat.

1980

23

Apollinaire Trepanned

remembers the red
poem hot from his head
in the palm of his hand.

As rubber gloves
lifted my lid
with my helmet, did
an uprush of doves

flutter the nurses? When
will the birds that filled
my green branches build
there again?

1969

Edward Thomas's Fob Watch

Face to face, hand in hand,
never a day apart
until the last day and
the wordless heart to heart.

2003

War Poet

facilis descensus Averno:
noctes atque dies patet atri ianua Ditis;
sed revocare gradum superasque evadere ad auras,
hoc opus, hic labor est.

Virgil, *Aeneid* VI, 126–29

Back to South Leigh for evensong
and, in the sermon, watched the long
arm of the sun restore the Doom
above the chancel arch. *Thy kingdom
come*, with a vengeance! The entrenched dead,
rising as Reveille sounded,
parted company. Sinners condemned
to join the chain-gang of the damned
recovered 'objects of desire'
and fell in for eternal fire.

I knew them, even naked – Smith,
Haynes, Adrian, Hill, Roberts (with
his hand restored) – my own lot, plus
the General. *He* had earned his place!
But then, herded with them downhill,
I was reprieved. Detailed for hell,
I heard beyond the traverse
an archangelic sentry's voice:
'Wiring party coming in.'

They came in without Adrian.

★

We never found him – never will –
with the 25-pounders still
pounding the waves of wire and mist.
We miss him in the morning most
when his Reveille, whistled, set
the blackbird on the parapet

26

Reveille-ing back.
                        Did another
one whistle over Golgotha?

                    ★

Are you still there – and still my love,
lighting a candle for me still?
I have been Absent Without Leave

almost from life itself, they tell
me, the good sisters, since Christophe
exhumed me from the house a shell

brought blazing down. The boy is deaf
and dumb, but lion-hearted! Hurt
his hands freeing me, dragging off

a burning rafter and the shirt
of Nessus. *St* Christophe saved me,
discovering a heart-beat, heart-

beat in the blackened turnip he
delivered to the convent door.
Dear love, I have no memory

of these things, *anything* before
the light, tidal not candlelight.
I was dissolved in what I saw –

for days, months, centuries it might
have been. Until in God's good time
or timelessness, the tide of light

began to ebb and I to climb
to consciousness, to tidal pain.
That also ebbed in God's good time

to leave me stranded, eyes open,
seeing only distant sails
tacking through fog. It cleared, and then

I saw white coifs between the isles
of broken castaways. One night,
a coif and candle came from miles

away. Something about the white
hand holding the white candle set
a fuse behind the eyes alight.

Lying there, trying to forget
the bad dreams, suddenly I knew
that somewhere there was something yet

to live for. Fuselight led me through
my ruined archives to a blaze
of recognition – nights and days with you.

★

Numbness and disbelief –
as Roberts in No Man's Land
felt, finding he had no hand
below a pumping sleeve.

Without you, I am learning
about death. It cannot be true
that you – you – you –
and my numbness turning

to anger. But however slow
the fire, however deep the seam,
it will burn out, they say, in time.
In time for what? Forgiveness? No.

Acceptance? How should I resign
myself to knowing that you lie
under another sky
in other arms than mine?

The bears you kept for company
sharing your bed when I could not,
the pair you christened You and Me –
our old Familiars – in what

new room do they keep company?
Your place or his place, and in what
position – bear or missionary?
Or are they banished to some spot

chillier than they used to know –
up on a shelf, facing the wall,
hearing no evil, seeing no
evil, speaking no evil at all?

Such delicacy I commend,
such reticence – but love is weak
and, lamentably, in the end
Orpheus will always turn and speak.

*

Heart, full as the moon
was full, a broken ring now,
an empty sky soon.

*

The things one remembers – a liking
for candles – *where* one remembers, and *why*.
Tuscany. A cracked clapper striking
the hour in a shimmering sky.

San Nicolo called me across the square
from sunlight to starlight, a glimmering
constellation of candles. Star-gazing there,
I lost – and found – myself remembering

candles beside our bed, cinnamon,
sandalwood spicing the air.
San Nicolo watched me light one
for you and might have heard a prayer:

If you should see her candles bloom
beside another bed that she
now shares, let her in an outer room
light one for me.

★

Back – for your wedding – to South Leigh.
The church was empty but for me
and overhead (as the saint says)
so great a cloud of witnesses.
Remember them? The Last Reveille
summoning sinners to the melée
at the mouth of hell?
                              Ached for the damned
that day as for myself, condemned
to witness what I hoped was joy:
vows, rings, exchanged; lips and hands joined
a world away. I should have sung
for you, but with my lyre unstrung
epithalamia were not
on hand. Instead, I wrote this note
by candle-light – one lit for you and
when it went out, I went too.

★

Whenever the child cried out at night,
he would be rescued by a blade of light,
a mother's paper and pencil. 'Draw
me the horror you say you saw,
and your drawing will drive it away.'
Your grown child heard that again today.
I was trying to escape, cutting a path
uphill in the sulphurous aftermath

of some Armageddon, sensed but not seen
in the valley where we had been.
No sound but the bark of a dog, somewhere
ahead or behind us, rasping the air
as we with our gasping, she and I.
Her voice then behind me: 'Look how the sky
lightens along the ridge. If we can keep
heading for that, who knows, we could sleep
in a happy valley.'
                              It was true –
the bright ridge a blade to the rescue.
I turned to take her hand, but as I did
her body, like a candle, melted
into smoke, a writhing ghost the wind
snatched from my arms.
                              Real or imagined
the animal cry that woke me? Hers
or mine? No exorcist answers
as I write this, and an Arctic light
uncovers the bedspread and the white pillow
warmed, through other nights, by one
whose smile was my sunrise. My un-
returning, subterranean sun.

                              ★

You again, blackbird! Welcome back –
as you were welcomed to a white
window-sill in the labour ward,
welcoming me to my first light.

No inkling of the mistress you
would herald, when you piped us up
to No Man's Land. She found me words
to shield the firestep

under fire, and afterwards
to pull me back, scorched but alive,
from other fires. Why should I
be granted a ticket of leave

if not to honour her and learn
from you – singing through rain or sun
your Edensong, till a dark wind
blows out the chestnut candles, one

by one?

2009

Goodbye to Wilfred Owen

killed, while helping his men
bring up duckboards, on the
bank of the Sambre Canal.

After the hot convulsion, this
cold struggle to break free – from whom?
I am not myself nor are his
hands mine, though once I was at home
with them. Pale hands his mother praised,
nimble at the keyboard, paler
now and still, waiting to be prised
from wood darker for their pallor.

Head down in a blizzard of shrapnel,
before the sun rose we had lost
more than our way. Disembodied
mist moves on the goose-fleshed canal,
dispersing slowly like the last
plumed exhalations of the dead.

War Song of the Embattled Finns
1939

Snow inexhaustibly
falling on snow! Those whom
we fight are so many,
Finland so small,
where shall we ever find room
to bury them all?

1964

A Letter from Berlin

My dear,
        Today a letter from Berlin
where snow – the first of '38 – flew in,
settled and shrivelled on the lamp last night,
broke moth wings mobbing the window. Light
woke me early, but the trams were late:
I had to run from the Brandenburg Gate
skidding, groaning like a tram, and sodden
to the knees. Von Neumann operates at 10
and would do if the sky fell in. They lock
his theatre doors on the stroke of the clock –
but today I was lucky: found a gap
in the gallery next to a chap
I knew just as the doors were closing. Last,
as expected, on Von Showmann's list
the new vaginal hysterectomy
that brought me to Berlin.

                 Delicately
he went to work, making from right to left
a semi-circular incision. Deft
dissection of the fascia. The blood-
blossoming arteries nipped in the bud.
Speculum, scissors, clamps – the uterus
cleanly delivered, the pouch of Douglas
stripped to the rectum, and the cavity
closed. Never have I seen such masterly
technique. 'And so little bleeding!' I said
half to myself, half to my neighbour.

                     'Dead',
came his whisper. 'Don't be a fool'
I said, for still below us in the pool
of light the marvellous unhurried hands
were stitching, tying the double strands
of catgut, stitching, tying. It was like
a concert, watching those hands unlock
the music from their score. And at the end

one half expected him to turn and bend
stiffly towards us. Stiffly he walked out
and his audience shuffled after. But
finishing my notes in the gallery
I saw them uncover the patient: she
was dead.
                I met my neighbour in the street
waiting for the same tram, stamping his feet
on the pavement's broken snow, and said:
'I have to apologize. She was dead,
but how did you know?' Back came his voice
like a bullet – 'saw it last month, twice.'

Returning your letter to an envelope
yellower by years than when you sealed it up,
darkly the omens emerge. A ritual wound
yellow at the lip yawns in my hand;
a turbulent crater; a trench, filled
not with snow only, east of Buchenwald.

1965

Wiedersehen

for Joachim Utz

Tom – and in time! I never thought you'd come
or not in time, since that's in short supply.
They can't plug an hourglass into my arm,
but no matter now. You're here, and I
must find the words whose loss cost me your love.
What do I know of loss? Do you deny
your 'unforgiving father' knowledge of love?
Of anything but hatred? When I tried
to stop you learning German, would not have
your *Freunde* in the house, your *Fräulein*, bride –
not even her – that was no hatred, or
no hatred of Germans. Sit beside
the bed. I'll tell you a story.
                                            The war
had reached the Rhineland and a riverbank
where a blown bridge knelt in the water.
The first soldier to reach it knelt and drank
and was shot in the head. A second, hit
lifting him, crashed in the river, sank.
Six crowded in a ditch. One raised his helmet
on a stick and it clanged like a bell
holed by a high-velocity bullet.
A sniper, and in front, among the rubble
once a village on the other shore.
The officer went left – then right – bent double
down the ditch, and gave his orders: 'Four
men, left – together at the ditch's end
dash for the farmhouse and return his fire;
two to go right – the ditch follows the bend
in the river, swim across, and ambush him.'
The Old'un led off his unblooded friend,
the Young'un, right. The bren snarled after them
and the sniper replied. Rounding his flank,
they came to the river. Rifles can't swim
so they strapped them each to a driftwood plank

37

and ferried them over. It was so cold,
the water and the wind on that scoured bank,
their fingers bled before they unbuckled
their guns and could move on – each covering
the other – to the kill, or to be killed.
Only a bird stirred in the lane, shivering
as they, sidling from tree to tree, shivered,
and then from doorway to doorway. Turning
into the square, the Old'un never heard
the shot that starred his face. The Young'un backed
against a door. It opened, and he entered
retching; from a reflex of a cracked
shop window, saw the church across the square,
its chancel smouldering, its belfry hacked
away, a tower beheaded, but there
above the parapet a moving head. Hatred
raised the rifle to the shoulder,
aligned the sights and braced the arm. Hatred,
hardly breathing, beckoned. As the muzzle leaped
the man stood up, and with his arms outspread
could have been crucified – until he stepped
into thin air.
                    He wore no uniform,
no bandolier. You would have thought he slept
but for his eyes, and his black coat was warm
to the touch of hands in search of papers. None,
except the photograph: he had his arm
around the waist of a woman,
who held a boy's hand and the flaxen plait
of a girl.
                    Why do you look at me like that?
In God's name, what are you staring at?

1984

At St Gennys

In their grandmothers' footsteps, the girls
of St Gennys played Grandmother's Footsteps
and skipped, skipped, in a blossom of curls
and pinafores, while the boys snatched caps
and shied them over the churchyard gate,
till Miss shook her bell to quell the noise
and call them in to chalk-stub and slate
through the door marked GIRLS and the door marked BOYS.

With a key from the cottage we let ourselves in
(through the door marked GIRLS) to the long room
empty since... Empty? Cupboard doors open
on a coiled adder, guardian of the tomb.
A gasp laughed off, seeing the eye unlit,
my sons drift out to swing on the farm gates.
And warily I lift the corselet
from the hoard, a stack of children's slates.

I cannot read the Book of the Dead,
but hear scribes breathing, a chalk edge
etching the darkness from which, now, a head
lifts, looking beyond the window-ledge,
the ivy tendril, and the churchyard wall –
to what enlightenment? How time translates
chalk-written names and tots up all
our stumbling numbers into frozen dates?

Not many, I think, learnt translation here.
But was there a sprouting boy who did not
look to that window, colouring its clear
glass with his dreams? What fish? What fairgrounds? What
sealed orders from the girls' sealed lips
sailed past the church tower, and what cargo
was there for them when their ships
came home? Their grandchildren would know.

Or would have known, had not three bachelors
of this parish dunged a field in France;
three more gone, weighted, to the fishes' jaws;
one fallen like a star. Five spinster aunts,
sometimes when tossing the sheaves from stook
to cart, would break off, brushing a strand
of hair back from their eyes, and look
out to cloud convoys making for the land.

1976

The Nutcracker

for Isaiah Berlin

My story? Yes, I got my story
though not the one I was assigned.
It was a Voyage of Discovery
all right, but of another kind.
The latest Russian Revolution
was no sooner known than it – *whoosh* – un-
corked Moscow like shaken champagne,
filled Red Square to the brim again
with chanting thousands. When Apollo
appeared on the balcony, they
let out a shout heard miles away.
He made a speech I couldn't follow
but knew would be a press release
before I had to write my piece.

A theme for Shostakovich: Russia's
Columbus, orbiting the earth
alone for 90 minutes, ushers
the space-age in. At such a birth
Siberian stars should sing hosannas,
not children with *Gagarin* banners.
Flags licked his face all afternoon.
Later, beneath a carnival moon,
I went to someone's celebration
and there, at the turn of a head,
a whisper, I was rocketed
beyond hope – dread – imagination –
I'm telling this the wrong way. I'm
afraid I must go back in time

before the war, to days we've chosen
not to discuss. Imagine me
emerging – into air like frozen
vodka – from the *wagon-lit*
at Moscow station. January

of 1938. A very
far cry from the *Champs Elysées*,
les croissants dans le petit café,
a pipe and *Le Temps*, a part in a
continuous historical play
I was helping to write all day,
white-tie reception, black-tie dinner,
five-star brandy and five-star dreams:
a canter in the *Bois*... *Maxim's*...

So there I was in a dim Chancery,
all day the very model of
a modern Second Secretary,
reviewing files on Molotov
or drafting, when the show-trial circus
began, reports on how the workers
of Krasnoyarsk had been betrayed.
Eyes in the courtroom were afraid
and not in the courtroom only,
but in the streets, the trams that hurled
them home at dusk and left the world
to darkness and the N.K.V.D.
I turned in early, took to bed
Memoirs from the House of the Dead.

A thunderous summer, a long winter,
though there'd be longer. Spain ablaze
and Britain refusing to inter-
vene. Now, it's not the last red days
of Barcelona I remember
so much as finding, in December,
a glint of green. Not in the park,
but in a studio after dark
where champagne bottles fountained freely,
toast after toast. Somebody said
'Tatyana'. Laughter, and a head
was turned. 'Tatyana Taraschvili.'
Her eyes were champagne-bottle green,
the greenest eyes I'd ever seen.

And her voice had a champagne sparkle
in it: 'You are a diplomat
of course.' My diplo-patriarchal
amour propre was piqued by that.
'And you?' I said. 'A fortune-teller?'
'No.' 'Actress?' 'No.' 'A teacher?' 'No.' 'Well, a
translator?' 'No.' The man beside
her smiled at her as she replied,
and picked up an accordion. Swaying
a little and tapping one toe,
he started playing – a low
slow pulse – advancing and delaying.
Tatyana said, 'Will you excuse
me please?' and stepped out of her shoes.

The drinkers and the talkers, hearing
the music, fell back to the wall
and she stepped forward into the clearing
and stopped, making no move at all.
What started as the first faint stirring
of summer wind, the murmuring
of birches, rocked the orchards, made
the barley sway. And she soon swayed.
Then glided off with small steps stitching
the edge of the clearing, white feet
obedient to the steady beat.
She was Daphne. She was bewitching!
The accordion caught its breath, changed key.
Apollo was bewitched – like me.

She danced a *pas de deux* with her shadow,
embroidering the smoky air
as if the law of gravity had no
imperial jurisdiction there,
but other winged heels crossed the meadow.
The music quickened. A tornado
all but plucked her off the ground,
spinning round and faster round
and faster round, with arms extended,
and every time I crossed her line

43

of vision, green eyes engaged mine.
When, with a chord, the whirlwind ended,
a storm of clapping shook the eaves
but not the laurel with two green leaves.

I had my answer. She was toasted
again, again, again. More chords,
and everybody danced, or most did.
A lamp was swaying and floor-boards
shuddered at Cossack leaps. My *Dashing
White Sergeant* sent their glasses smashing
against the wall, but there were more.
We gravitated to the floor
as the liquor found its level
and launched a song with a song in tow
like Volga barges deep and slow.
Tomorrow could go to the devil!
Meanwhile, champagne, accordion –
On with the dance! Tatyana? Gone.

Prince Charming had a hangover
the size of an onion dome
and no tall footman to discover
the barefoot Cinderella's home.
But *was* she – champagne's a deceiver –
Natasha Rostov *rediviva*?
I had to find her to know that.
Some mornings after, as I sat
considering coffee and a stiff tot
of whisky, came a letter: *Dear
dashing white British Grenadier,
have you outgrown toy soldiers? If not,
come with this ticket and enjoy
the Nutcracker at the Bolshoi.*

I went of course, and when the curtain
swept back a century to show
the candled Christmas tree, I'm certain
no child at the darkened window
so caught its breath. 'Is it her? Is it her?'

I asked of each elegant visitor
in velvet and long white gloves.
The children eddied round like doves
with Masha in the lead. And Masha – for
all the turbulent cascade
of hair remembered in a braid – was
unmistakably Natasha.
Watching the wave of her hair,
I knew she knew that I was there.

At midnight in her dream – or was it
my dream? – when all the guests had gone,
the Mouse King marched from the closet
and with his brigand battalion
attacked the grenadiers. Surrounded,
outnumbered, the toy soldiers sounded
their trumpets, fought and fell, until
all but the Nutcracker lay still.
They cut him down, had stabbed and kicked him,
when Masha flashed across the room
and with a well-aimed slipper boom-
eranged the King. Raising his victim,
her kisses and her tears transformed
the wooden limbs her body warmed.

Her prince I didn't warm to greatly –
the rippled hair, insistent smile.
He handled her too intimately
for someone known such a short while,
but he danced well – she danced superbly –
and their *rapport* did not disturb me
for, as she danced with him, I thought
she danced for me. Then as he brought
her, gliding in his magic troika
through waltzing snowflakes, waltzing flowers,
I thought 'the Last Waltz could be ours'.
Naive! But after the Bolshoi cur-
tain closed, Tchaikovsky in my head
sent me waltzing home to bed.

Next day – one of those Saturdays a
man feels the world and the flesh in tune –
my face met a waltzing razor,
my coffee a waltzing spoon.
I reined my pen in as it wrote her
a note that showed not one iota
of what I wanted it to say,
but *Thank you... magical... and may
I have the pleasure, etc.,
on New Year's Eve?* She came, her bloom
irradiating my grey room.
The bortsch was good, the wine was better,
a candle flame danced in the draught,
pirouetting when we laughed.

How far that little candle... laughter...
Tatyana's exuberant mime!
We talked the Old Year out, and after
our glasses had sounded their chime,
we talked the New Year in. I drove her
home when the night was almost over;
or almost home, lest we should meet
the N.K.V.D. in her street.
'Next time,' she said, 'I'll do the cooking.'
Leant over, kissed me. The car door
slammed in the wind. She turned the cor-
ner, collar up, without looking
back, and before I could move on,
her footprints, filled with snow, had gone.

Another wait, another letter.
Five days, four evenings – three, two, one –
returning to Tchaikovsky's meta-
morphosis, a transformation
no more miraculous, no greater
than mine, to other music, later.
After my Bollinger's salute
to her triumphant *boeuf en croûte*,
when first the electricity
and then the candle failed, what could

we do? At least the stove had wood
enough. When snow had put the city
to bed, what could we do, discov-
ering (what else?) we were in love?

With that, our music changed key, quickened.
We danced through January, danced
through February. Birch buds thickened –
and headlines, as Hitler advanced
on Prague. We danced, one night in March, a
snowflake waltz to a borrowed *dacha* –
my Humber waltzing down the road
to Peredelkino. It snowed
all that weekend. We didn't bother,
but stayed luxuriously in bed.
Ourselves an open book, we read
Eugene Onegin to each other
and thanked our stars that they were not
Eugene and his Tatyana's lot.

How could we doubt, ecstatic lovers,
that ours were dancing night and day
in some Chagall-like zone above us
as April melted into May,
snow into blossom? Every Sunday
we woke in a world of Sugar Candy
at Peredelkino, and there
forgot that other stars elsewhere
were goose-stepping to music harsher
than ours. In the world we left behind,
Hitler and Mussolini signed
a treaty, Germany and Russia
announced a non-aggression pact,
and then the fear became the fact.

But still we danced – despite the writing
emerging on the Chancery wall
where moving fingers flagged the fighting –
until, in '41, the wal-
tzing stopped. In the blink of an eyelid,

a telegram, two worlds collided.
I was recalled. What could I do?
I could resign, and did. I knew
a London newspaper that wanted
a Man in Moscow, and applied.
I had (I said) sources inside
the Kremlin. So I was appointed,
bar the formalities, and flew
to England for an interview.

There was no interview. I landed
as Russia caught fire from the Black
Sea to the Baltic. I was stranded –
no job, no visa, no way back –
conscripted, between ice and fire.
My letters to Tatyana (via
the diplomatic bag) brought no
reply. Her footprints filled with snow,
snow burying a U-boat chaser
off Archangel, the snows of four
pitiless winters. When the war
was over, I went back to trace her.
Found nothing but a bombed-out flat.
Came home. Found you. And that was that –

until this week, that celebration.
The turn of a head. Those eyes.
My name with an intonation
not heard for 20 years. Replies
to 20 years' interrogation:
'Leningrad… through the siege… starvation…
the survivors had someone for whom
to survive.' She looked across the room
and smiled – at *him*. Daybreak and tidal
wave! Drowning, I saw us again –
dancing, cooking, drinking champagne,
reading, waking – and then as I'd al-
ways dreamt we'd be: husband and wife,
father and mother. Child. A life

usurped. I saw him, the usurper,
their *pas de deux* a shuffle ov-
er snow, their scavenging for supper,
resuscitating a cold stove.
I saw them in the white nights, under
one blanket, hearing the guns thunder
and plaster trickle down the wall.
Untrue. I saw nothing at all,
heard nothing, would not taste those kisses
and tears. I was lost in the wake
of their lives. Then felt Tatyana take
my hand and heard her saying: 'This is
your son.' So there it is, my story.
And I'm so happy. I'm so sorry.

1988

A poem about Poems About Vietnam

The spotlights had you covered [thunder
in the wings]. In the combat zones
and in the Circle, darkness. Under
the muzzles of the microphones
you opened fire, and a phalanx
of loudspeakers shook on the wall;
but all your cartridges were blanks
when you were at the Albert Hall.

Lord George Byron cared for Greece,
Auden and Cornford cared for Spain,
confronted bullets and disease
to make their poems' meaning plain;
but you – by what right did you wear
suffering like a service medal,
numbing the nerve that they laid bare,
when you were at the Albert Hall?

The poets of another time –
Owen with a rifle-butt
between his paper and the slime,
Donne quitting Her pillow to cut
a quill – knew that in love and war
dispatches from the front are all.
We believe them, they were there,
when you were at the Albert Hall.

Poet, they whisper in their sleep
louder from underground than all
the mikes that hung upon your lips
when you were at the Albert Hall.

1968

A Portrait of Robert Capa

Three eyes in the mirror
behind the bar (one of them shut
since five o'clock) burn and burn out
    in time to the mortar

    like a severed vein
ejaculating on the night
jet after rhythmic jet of light.
    'How did it go?' The brain

    unreels its images
frame by frame: holding to the flash
troops kneeling by a stream to wash
    unfamiliar faces;

    boots on a white road show
their teeth; a corporal on his back
plays with a puppy and a stick.
    'Robert, what'll you do

    when the war is over?'
The third eye lifted in a mute
rejoinder to the gun's salute,
    blinks at the mirror

    before the concussion
succeeds the flash. 'I cover
a war that will never
    be lost, never be won.'

1965

Kathmandu–Kodari

They are building a road out of Kathmandu –
sixty-three miles to be cut with the spade
and five tall bridges to be made
with baskets of cement and bamboo

scaffolding. They are building a road
to Kodari, a high road to be met
with ceremony in Tibet
by the Chungking-Lhasa-Kodari road.

What will they carry, these five tall bridges?
Coolies trudging northward under bales of rice
or troop-filled lorries
travelling south? Periwigged like judges

the Himalayas watch the road-gangs labour.
Today, though the road-gangs seldom look up,
Kangchenjunga wears a black cap:
and the wind from Tibet sweeps like a sabre.

1964

Skyhorse

And I looked, and behold a pale horse:
and his name that sat on him was Death.

Revelation 6:8

It is a peculiarity of the Germans to seek omens and warnings from horses. They are kept at public expense in the same groves and woods, white and untouched by any human labour; after they have been harnessed to the sacred chariot, the priest and the king or chieftain of the tribe accompany them and take note of their neighs and snortings. No portent is more trusted, not only by the common people, but by the aristocracy and the priests; for they consider themselves to be the gods' servants, but the horses actually their confidants.

Tacitus: *Germania*, 10, 3–5

Before the gods that made the gods
    Had seen their sunrise pass,
The White Horse of the White Horse Vale
    Was cut out of the grass.

G.K. Chesterton: *The Ballad of the White Horse*

…that high horse riderless,
Though mounted in that saddle Homer rode…

W.B. Yeats: 'Coole Park and Ballylee, 1931'

The year of the horse

began auspiciously:
the whitest stallion
in the Sacred Grove
mounting the whitest mare.

When prophecies followed,
the praise-singer offered
a millennial ode
to the whitest mare.

The first priest of
the White Horse
tells his son of his
commission,
*c.*1000 BC

When the skyhorse jumped out of the sky
when his eye
when his breath
when his teeth
death.

Firebreath then
but no firelight
and women talking.
  – Three days dead
but no deathsmell.
  – Whose death, woman? I said.
Their answer only the sound
as of does in flight
of feet shaking the ground.
Four feet, then many,
and voices I knew well
came near and spoke my name.
  – We saw the skyhorse claim him
with his hooves, his teeth,
and yet he moves.
  – And speaks. What cave
darkens your face?
  – No cave, brother. This is the hill
where you and the skyhorse met,
where he gave us fire,
where he set the mark
of his hoof on your head,
making your eyes dark,
ash-white your hair.

Oh then I heard a voice
I knew and did not know
as mine cry
                Skyhorse,
stargrazer, firebringer,
if you require my eyes
in tribute, gladly

I give them. I will be
your praise-singer.
But if, bestowing light
and dark, you light my eyes
as you have lighted fire,
I and my sons will whiten
the hill's head with your mark,
shadowing your shadow
for all the tribes to praise.

And when the day's eye opened,
mine could see it shine.

Priest and poet,
*c.*970 BC

The skyhorse calls
for his bondman,
his priest, who lies
in his shadow
and will not rise
until we let
his spirit go.

The trees add their
lament to ours.
He was their friend,
singing their praise.
In tribute now
his trees let fall
a branch, a bough.

So we must go
and gather them,
men shouldering
the gifts of oak
and ash, children
a holly branch
or mistletoe.

And as we build
the horseman's pyre
see the pictures
I shall sing. –
The horse stamping
his hill, bringing
his people fire.

The horse darkens
a man with light,
a praise-singer
he makes his own.
The man shaping
what his eyes saw.
Flint scraping bone.

The skyhorse leaps
from a white bone
to a burnt hill.
His horseman sows
it with white stones.
On the burnt earth
a starhorse glows.

Skinning the hill
between the stones,
the praise-singer
honours the horse
that honours us,
our guardian
and firebringer.

Bring me a seed
of fire to sow.
It will take root
and its flowers tell
whose spirit goes
to the great cave.
Father, go well.

Poet of the
shield-wall,
AD 871

... a boy on a brown horse
came to the King's tent, and Ethelred called
for Alfred, his brother, and all the thanes.
While the King was in council, word went out
that his cook had seen a silver penny
the boy had been given for bringing news
of Danes on the Ridgeway. King Ethelred,
after the earls had spoken, said: 'We are all
of one mind. We march at cockcrow
and the Lord of Hosts shall lead us.
Tonight, let the armourer look to his anvil,
put sword to whetstone, rivet the shield.'

Firelight set the farm cocks crowing
when the sun still slept under the hill,
nor had it shaken the stars from its hair
until we were mustered and on the march.
The Prince rode ahead of us. His horse
was a white candle in the dark wood.
Then the laggard sun rose, drying the dew
on weapons that soon would again be wet.
On Ashdown, a shield and another shield
flashed not far from the crest. Prince Alfred
turned in his saddle and shouted:
'Shall the heathen stand between this white horse
and his ancient sire?' The army's answer,
hurled round the hills, reached the Danes
as thunder.

They were drawn up
in two divisions. 'Let us do likewise',
the earls said, 'when King Ethelred comes.'
'The Danes do not know he comes. Divide
and strike now,' the Prince replied. Two shield-walls
he ordered, setting old soldiers
among the young. When all were in place,
'Poet,' he said, 'as we step forward,
sing us the lay of the fight at Aclea.'

So I gave them the lay as the green gap
narrowed and the first spears flew.
Eadric, my shire-fellow, dropped at my side.
When the shield-walls clashed, the Prince's sword
was the first to bite. Like a wild boar
he gored earl Sidroc. That was the old earl,
whose son advancing to avenge his sire
bowed his horned helmet. Blood blinded him.
Nor did our earls wield their weapons less fiercely.
Godwin cut down three Danes with gold torques
before he was felled by an evil axe.
With him his brother's son, Wulfstan, fell.
A hard hill we climbed but Heaven's King,
to whom be praise, heard his champion's prayer
at mass that morning. When Ethelred's men
came to the war-play, they came without warning.
Viking eyes were elsewhere as their enemy
struck. We heard then a stallion
utter its war-cry. 'Hear the White Horse,'
earl Aelfwine shouted, and all at once
the heathen broke ranks and ran …

Wandering Scholar,
13th century

May morning and a marvel
I climbed a hill to see,
when hedge choirs were singing
of love, but not to me.

The marvel, a white stallion,
where choirs of cherubim
or skylarks were singing
of love, but not to him.

I grieved that his creator
did not take from him there
a rib, when he was sleeping,
to make him a white mare,

as my creator made me –
O Christe, ubi sunt
that hand and fragrant breast,
that mouth and flagrant cunt?

Another man that morning
could answer, but not I
alone on White Horse hill
under a singing sky,

thanking my creator
for hedge choirs, lark and linnet,
for making a green world
with such white marvels in it.

Antiquary,
18th century Gentleman-Commoner, drawn by the lure
Of paquet-boat, post-chaise, and the Grand Tour,
Let Tully be your tutor. 'Call complete
No scholar's learning that is not replete
With knowledge of his native land.' You seek
Antiquities. Must they be marble, Greek
Or Roman? Grander monuments of stone
Await you in a landscape of your own.
See Hadrian's Wall before you seek his Tomb.
His works should be your study, not his doom:
Imperial verses that outlast the bronze
Testudo, eagles and centurions.
Archon of Athens, he was Homer's slave:
An oarsman furrowing the wine-dark wave,
A charioteer, Achilles in the field
Astride a Trojan dazzled by his shield.
He saw with Homer's eyes, but not his own,
The walls of Ilium. We could have shown
Him ramparts overlooking Uffington
As old as those and closer to the sun,
A windy castle that his legions held
Against our fathers, where our fathers felled
The Danish King. The White Horse that red day
Trampled his Raven, and the Norsemen lay
In broken ranks, a banquet for the crows.
Beyond the castle gate, the hillside shows
A people's tribute to a warrior prince,
A White Horse groomed and venerated since.
A nobler horse than Homer's timber mare,
A nobler shade than Hector, unsung, there
Await their chronicler and celebrant.
Look not to Italy or the Levant.
Let your Parnassus be our White Horse hill.
Your muses comb their hair by Letcombe Mill.

Rifleman
(discharged)
52nd Regiment,
18 June 1832

Whur else ud I be on this uv all days
But yer, givin' God an' 'is 'oss-ship thanks
Fer seventeen yurs an' a sweeter smoke
Than singed me gizzard in the soddin' ranks

Uv riflemen an' barley? 'On thee feeyut!'
The Colonel said, 'An' let they chassers choke
On a Baker's dozen!' 'Alf a dozen an'
They staggert, two more an' they broke.

Out uv the column, over they swothes,
A riderless white 'oss gallopt away.
Boney's pony, us said, leadin' our charge!
God, 'oss, an' baggonet wun us the day.

Not Boney's 'oss, but one sin in a dream
That night. One at 'oose feeyut I ust to play.
One at 'oose feeyut I smokes a pipe
Wi' ole ghosts ev'ry yur on this day.

Mother, 1899   Was it for this we climbed the hill,
You with your hurt pride, I with my shame –
A well-scoured wedding ring and still
No child to bear your name?

Was it for this the aching heart,
The prayers, the potions, the remorse,
And you playing the stallion's part
That night under the White Horse?

For this, the anxious hope, the pains,
The truants all day out on the hill
Fighting battles, Saxons and Danes,
The king on his horse – our Will?

Would we have climbed there had we known
What the Colonel's letter would say?
... *At Elandslaagte ... your son...*
Under his gallant grey...

Midsummer Day, 1905

Colonel and others,
1905

1000 hrs. Bandsmen arrive
For practice at the White Horse Inn.
1200 hrs. Bandsmen depart
For Castle in Bandmaster's cart.

Under the eye of the sovereign
Sun, the White Horse Regulars stand
Waving a hat, waving a hand
At the Kingston Lisle United
      (the White Horse Inn's) Brass Band.

1300 hrs. Refreshment
To be taken in Bandsmen's tent.
1330 hrs. Review
By Colonel Hippisley
                there
Fulfilling at the Midsummer Fair
A major's dream in the Karroo
Of J.P. Sousa, Gilbert and
Sullivan ... played in a green land
By the Kingston Lisle United
      (Hippisley's Own) Brass Band.

Farmers in uniform, we set
Our lips to mouthpieces once wet
In Africa (and when the war
Was over, the band disbanded,
Sold to our Colonel for
A song). Can the Roman dead
Hear us today, as we stand
Our ground on the ramparts they manned
Before the Kingston Lisle United
      (Berkshire's Best) Brass Band?

The Colonel's pride and his despair –
His band performing at the Fair
Buttercup in buttonhole
And no more sense of decent style
Than milkmaids round a maypole.

                                    But
When Uffington and Kingston Lisle
Tug-of-war teams meet hand to hand,
The crowd's pulse is the pulse of the band,
The Kingston Lisle United
        (Morrell & Sons') Brass Band.

After the wrestling and the last race,
'Stripping the Willow' takes the place
Of 'British Grenadiers', a rasped
Match reddens a bonfire. Through
Its sparks, they circle two by two,
The strangers and the sweethearts, clasped
Or very shyly hand in hand,
Be-Sousa'd and be-Sullivanned
By the Kingston Lisle United
        (Midsummer Night's) Brass Band.

… 11, 12 … the church clocks chime
Across the valley. Fanfare time
For Fortune's waggon-wheel, old wood
Sheathed in new straw, blazing downhill
In pursuit of the sun. How will
It come to rest? Foretelling good
Or ill? And what has Fortune planned
For us – who can scarcely stand –
The Kingston Lisle United
        (Hip, hip, Hippisley's Own) Brass Band?

They say the White Horse knows, and neighs
For good luck, snorts for bad. We may's
Well ask. A fortune for a tune,
Played just for him, played in his ear.
Lie back and read the stars…

                          You hear
A sound? No? Must have dropped off. Soon
Be dawn. United we shall stand –
If sometimes with a helping hand –
The Kingston Lisle United
            (The White Horse Vale's) Brass Band.

Homeguard, Ironic really, that men should have scoured
1940   The horse — men with our names — since it was scored
           Above Uffington, only for our spades
           To bury it: a king's emblem raised
           To comfort his folk, discomfort his foes,
           Lowered into one of the down's long barrows
           Lest the *Luftwaffe* set a course
           For Birmingham by the lie of our horse.

           No eye in England has seen so much:
           Men in skins, men in helmets, the slow march
           Of stars across the millennia,
           A new star in the east, and many
           A falling star — none, I dare say, as bright
           As the Messerschmitt that came down last night,
           Comet-tail scorching the tree tops, to land
           Where legend says the Danes made their last stand.

           Did a wind like this that ruffles your mane
           Bring you the taunts of axemen and swordsmen
           As it did the death-rattle of the plane?
           Only ash and an iron cross remain
           Of the pilot. We'll put him to bed
           When we've billeted you with the older dead.
           There'll be many more like that poor Kraut,
           And when we've dug them in, we'll dig you out.

Ex-homeguard,
1946

'You dug him in,' they said, 'you dig him out.
You know where he is.' That hurt, but they
Couldn't have known and I couldn't explain.
And if I had known what I know today,
I wouldn't have said, standing here in the rain,
'There'll be many more like that poor Kraut.'

The spade that buried him can't resurrect
A German airman known unto God,
But since our Dresden news came through
I've given his grave a flower or two,
Hoping some German might not neglect
An English airman known unto God.

Wandering
Scholar,
1999/2000

Setting foot on the hill, on living grass sprung
from grasses trodden by how many feet
grassed over since the horse was young,
I followed again the glimmering line
of a *calligramme* inscribed in chalk
through the last dark of '99.

I thought I should see from the horse's eye
a blazing constellation at my feet,
the valley mirroring the sky,
but the bonfire-makers were all at home,
watching the little people at their games
under a magic mushroom dome.

Would there be bells? Woolstone church held its
                                        tongue.
Midnight was zero hour. The Ridgeway air
shuddered under buffeting
flashes and crashes. Star-shells. Very lights.
I might have been dug in on Vimy Ridge
or bunkered on the Golan Heights.

I lay down by the horse to watch the show,
masque of a murderous century,
but a mist rolled up from below,
rolled up and over me. 'Call me Ishmael',
witness to the tremor, the rumbling sound,
the breaching not of a whale

but a white horse. Lifting its lucent head
it turned a terrible eye to mine,
and a voice at my ear said
'The skyhorse calls for his bondman, his priest.'
So I straddled its back, took hold of its mane,
as the marvellous beast

rose to its feet and through the clouds. Ahead
of us, Black Mountains … Irish Sea … The wind

was stitched with voices, one that said:
'Look at the stars! Look, look up at the skies!
O look at all the fire-folk sitting in the air!'
One whispering: 'Cast a cold eye

On life, on death. Horseman, pass by!'
                                 We passed
at such a pace – the great stride scissoring
the fabric of the dark so fast –
and such a height that the Atlantic shrank
to a water-jump for a white horse.
And I heard from the further bank,

above the static and the storms, the trace
of other voices, one a woman's,
on the obsidian disc of space:
'I, like the Earth this season, mourn in black,
My Sun is gone so far in's zodiac.'
And I said to myself, we *chase*

the sun – over this sunless continent,
these growling glaciers, voiceless snows, a grey
then a celadon sea. Fast as the sun went,
the horse went faster, from Arctic night
to Burmese afternoon, the Arakan
seen as from a satellite.

There, miles above the mountain tops
I heard a young man say:
'Across scorched hills and trampled crops
The soldiers straggle by.
History staggers in their wake.
The peasants watch them die.'

India was a green leaf on a blue sea …
Arabia the jawbone of a lion …
that puckered scar, Gallipoli,
haunted with voices. One I knew:
'Farmers in uniform – much frayed –
here at Cape Helles we parade

without our instruments.'
                          They never heard
what I would hear above the isles of Greece,
a distant, whispered,
'Seek out – less often sought than found –
a soldier's grave.' 'We didn't have to seek,'
said someone from a killing-ground

closer to home. 'I am the enemy
you killed, my friend ...' 'At Dunkirk I
rolled in the shallows, and the living trod
across me for a bridge ...'
                          White cliffs we crossed
in the wake of the sun then waking larks
along the Downs' familiar crest.

And there I heard a voice
I knew and did not know
as mine singing below:
'*O Christe, ubi sunt*
that hand and fragrant breast,
that mouth and flagrant cunt?

Another man that morning
could answer, but not I
alone on White Horse hill
under a singing sky.'
And so it was. I found
myself – as the horse went to ground –

on my back in long grass, surrounded
by voices interwoven with the wind:
that of a horseman who founded
a tribe singing a lay that extolled
the horse, as I walked down to Uffington
and into a future not foretold.

2002

Self-Portrait in Snow

for Tom Fairfax

Repainting the picture-window
from a winter palette, the wind
adds pointillist touches of snow.

It has lowered and darkened
pillow-case clouds. Eiderdown
brush-strokes whiten the island

(low left) but not the river, brown
as the drover's coat of the man
on the bridge. He's looking down-

stream. Looking at what? I can
remember summers seen from there,
high noons before the snow began

to settle, all year, on his hair.
He turns. I know him. He knows me.
Our eyes meet, look away – to stare

upstream – at what? We cannot see
for snow, and now an old toast drifts
unlooked-for into memory:

Gentlemen, when the barrage lifts!

2009

Notes

'The Anzac Sonata'

The Bluff. The most southerly point of the South Island of New Zealand..

'Edward Thomas's Fob Watch'

Stopped by the blast of the German shell that killed him at 7.36 a.m. on 9 April, Easter Monday, 1917.

'Skyhorse'

None of the chalk figures of England has excited so much interest as the mysterious, dragon-like creature sprawling along the edge of the downs at Uffington. So different from all the other white horses and so obviously very much older than they are, it seems to present a challenge and demand an explanation. Who made it? When? Why? Archaeologists have now answered the second of these questions asked by Morris Marples (in his book *White Horses and Other Hill Figures*, 1949, p. 28). Optically stimulated luminescence dating of samples from the White Horse's V-shaped chalk-filled trench show it to have been cut approximately 3,000 years ago. Poems 1 and 2 offer hypothetical answers to Marple's first and third questions.

The most detailed account of the battle of Ashdown in AD 871 is that of the monk Asser. See *Alfred the Great: Asser's Life of King Alfred and other contemporary sources,* translated with an Introduction and Notes by Simon Keynes and Michael Lapidge, 1983.

Aclea. In AD 851, King Aethelwulf and an army drawn from all over Wessex defeated a large Danish force at Aclea (a site now identified with Ockley in Surrey).

Wandering Scholar. The classic account of the medieval *Vagantes*, their Latin love songs and spring songs is Helen Waddell, *The Wandering Scholars*, 7th edn (revised), 1934.

Tully. Marcus Tullius, 106–43 BC, Roman senator, better known as Cicero.

Hadrian. Publius Aelius Hadrianus, AD 76–138, was elected archon of

74

Athens in AD 111 or 112 and, as poet and soldier, may be presumed an admirer of Homer. He visited Britain in AD 121 or 122, when Emperor of Rome, and ordered the building of what came to be known as Hadrian's Wall. He was buried in the mausoleum he had built in Rome.

A windy castle. The ancient camp, known as Uffington Castle, on the west of the downs above the White Horse.

On 18 June 1815, at the Battle of Waterloo, the Light Brigade, of which the 52nd Regiment formed a part, drove Napoleon's Chasseurs across a cornfield in a violent attacking manoevre. See Elizabeth Longford: *Wellington: The Years of the Sword*, pp. 477–78 for a full account of the battle.

'oss. Horse.

feeyut. Feet.

chassers. Chasseurs.

Baker's Dozen. The men of the 52nd Regiment, the Oxfordshire Light Infantry, were armed with Baker rifles.

swothes. Swathes.

Boney's Pony. At Waterloo, Napoleon was riding his white charger.

Elandslaagte. On one of the few occasions when British cavalry were committed in the Anglo-Boer War, a squadron each of the 5th Lancers and the 5th Dragoon Guards charged a Boer stronghold at Elandslaagte ('Elands Leap'), Natal, on 21 October 1899, killing or wounding most of its defenders.

Colonel Hippisley. William Henry Hippisley, 1855–1908, served in the Zulu Campaign of the South African War. Retiring to the village of Sparsholt at the foot of White Horse Hill, he kitted out the Kingston Lisle United Brass Band at his own expense.

Morrell & Sons. Oxfordshire brewers since 1782.

a bonfire. A reference to the Midsummer Eve bonfires around which young villagers would dance, leaping across them for good luck. A burning cartwheel would be rolled from a hilltop and, 'if it reached the valley still burning, to be quenched in river or pond', it was thought that 'Destiny would smile' (Laurence Whistler, *The English Festivals*, 1947, pp. 166–67).

In 1940, the White Horse, a familiar landmark to German bombers, was turfed over.

calligramme. Guillaume Apollinaire (1880–1918) called his 'shaped poems' *calligrammes*.

'*Call me Ishmael*'. The opening sentence of Herman Melville's *Moby-Dick*.

'*Look at the stars!*'. G.M. Hopkins, 'The Starlight Night', lines 1–2.

'*Cast a cold eye*'. W.B. Yeats, 'Under Ben Bulben', lines 92–94.

'*I, like the Earth this season*'. Anne Bradstreet, 'A Letter to Her Husband, Absent upon Public Employment', lines 7–8.

'*Across scorched hills*'. Alun Lewis, 'The Peasants', lines 9–12.

'*Seek Out*'. Lord Byron, 'On This Day I Complete my Thirty-Sixth Year', lines 37–38.

'*I am the enemy*'. Wilfred Owen, 'Strange Meeting', line 70.

'*At Dunkirk*'. Sidney Keyes, 'The Foreign Gate', lines 218–20.

'Self-Portrait in Snow'
On 28 June 1916, the officers of the King's Own Yorkshire Light Infantry were summoned for a final drink before going into battle. Captain Haswell stepped forward and, raising his glass, said: 'Gentlemen, I give you the toast of the King's Own Yorkshire Light Infantry, and in particular the 9th Battalion of the Regiment' – a slight pause – 'Gentlemen, when the barrage lifts.' Of those present, twenty-four went into action next day in the attack on Fricourt: twelve were killed, including Haswell. Three afterwards died of wounds, eight others were wounded, and only one was untouched.